STREAKS OF

BATIKS

FABRIC-INSPIRED QUILTS

Sandra L. Holzer

 American Quilter's Society

P.O. Box 3290 • Paducah, KY 42002-3290
Fax 270-898-1173 • e-mail: orders@AQSquilt.com

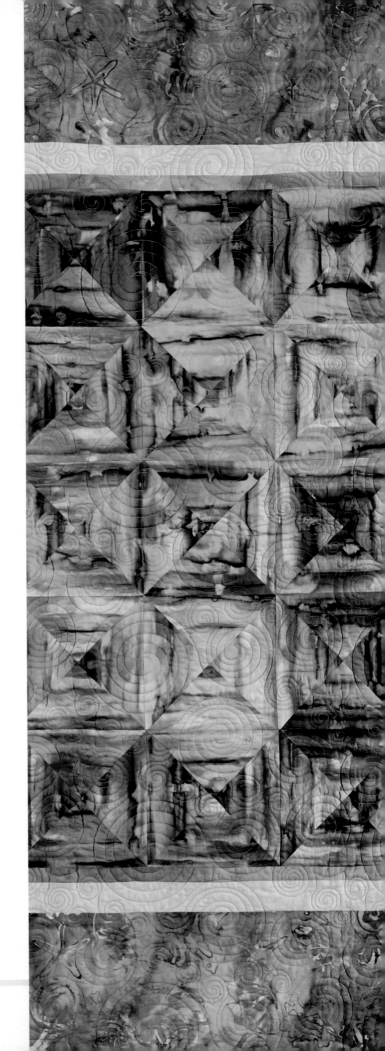

Located in Paducah, Kentucky, the American Quilter's Society (AQS) is dedicated to promoting the accomplishments of today's quilters. Through its publications and events, AQS strives to honor today's quiltmakers and their work and to inspire future creativity and innovation in quiltmaking.

EXECUTIVE EDITOR: ELAINE BRELSFORD
BOOK EDITOR: KATHY DAVIS
COPY EDITOR: CHRYSTAL ABHALTER
GRAPHIC DESIGN: ELAINE WILSON
COVER DESIGN: MICHAEL BUCKINGHAM
QUILT PHOTOGRAPHY: DAVID STANSBURY, UNLESS OTHERWISE STATED

Additional copies of this book may be ordered from the American Quilter's Society, PO Box 3290, Paducah, KY 42002-3290, or online at www.AmericanQuilter.com.

Text © 2013, Author, Sandra L. Holzer
Artwork © 2013, American Quilter's Society

Library of Congress Cataloging-in-Publication Data

HOLZER, SANDRA L.
    STREAKS OF BATIKS : FABRIC-INSPIRED QUILTS / BY SANDRA L. HOLZER.
        PAGES CM
    SUMMARY: "SANDRA SHOWS YOU HOW TO CUT AND SEW STRIPS FOR A SIMPLE, WASTE-FREE METHOD TO CREATE QUILT BLOCKS. ONE EASY TECHNIQUE GIVES YOU A LIFETIME OF DESIGN POSSIBILITIES, AND THE SEWING IS SIMPLICITY ITSELF. USE THESE VERSATILE BLOCKS FOR: ART QUILTS, APPLIQUÉ BACKGROUNDS, QUILT BORDERS, AND INTERESTING BACKINGS"– PROVIDED BY PUBLISHER.
    ISBN 978-1-60460-057-5
    1. PATCHWORK–PATTERNS. 2. STRIP QUILTING–PATTERNS. 3. BATIK. I. TITLE.
    TT835.H55624 2013
    746.46–DC23
                        2013019107

COVER: SILK FLOWERS, detail. Full quilt shown on page 12.
TITLE PAGE: BARNYARD, detail. Full quilt shown on page 73.

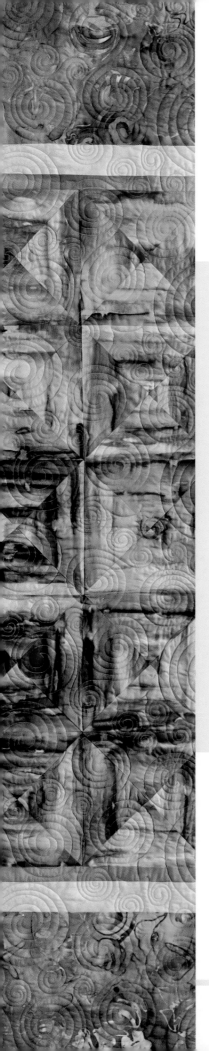

Dedication & Acknowledgments

This book is dedicated to my family: children, Kim and Mike, and husband, Tom. I acknowledge Mike for his ability to take my completed blocks and arrange them to create a balanced and cohesive unit for my early quilts. I thank Kim for her technical guidance and constructive criticism. I am grateful to both Kim and Mike for sharing their technical computer knowledge and their assistance with editing the book. Tom should be cited for patiently waiting outside various quilt shops as I frequently exceeded my time allotment and for encouraging me to travel to national quilting shows and develop my own quilting style.

I also wish to acknowledge my deceased father, Arthur H. Brown, who taught me as a young girl the mechanics of a sewing machine and how to use it.

This dedication would not be complete without voicing praise for Doryne Pederzani of Happy Valley Machine Quilting in Northampton, Massachusetts, for her skilled quilting of all of my quilts in this book. With her artistic abilities and willingness to experiment, these quilts were transformed from flat surfaces to meaningful artful expressions.

OPPOSITE: SWIRLS, detail. Full quilt shown on page 78.

Table of Contents

Streaks of Batiks. 7

  Fabric Selection. 7

  Quarter-Square Triangles from Strips

    versus Squares 10

Streaks of Batiks Quilt Master Plan 12

  Supply List. 12

  Yardage Requirements. 12

  Tools 14

  Cutting the Pieces. 14

  Streaks of Batiks Cutting Technique 15

  Placement of Triangles 16

  Constructing the Blocks. 18

  Arranging the Blocks 19

  Special Consideration When

    Setting Blocks On-Point 20

  Choosing Borders for the Quilt Blocks 22

  Quilt Back 22

  Quilting 24

  Finishing the Quilt. 25

Quilts 27

  HEART BEAT 28

  IRIS 32

  RIVER BED. 36

  LEX'S GARDEN 40

  GRAZING TURTLES 48

  ORNAMENTATION. 56

Piecing Border and Binding Strips. 64

Sleeve for Hanging 65

Binding the Quilt. 67

General Quilt Cleaning Directions. 71

Quilt Documentation. 72

  BRYNN ELIZABETH KLEINER'S QUILT 74

  JODHPUR'S GIFT. 75

Gallery 76

About the Author 79

OPPOSITE: FIREFLY, detail. Full quilt shown on page 21.

Streaks of Batiks

Make just one quarter-square triangle quilt using the *Streaks of Batiks* technique and you will never look at linear prints, stripes, and streaked batik fabrics the same way again. These fabrics can be cut into multiple triangles to create traditional, contemporary, or art quilts. The technique will yield blocks for bold and vibrant art quilts, form borders, or can be combined to create an interesting background for appliqué. The simple fabric selection, template-free cutting, and straight-line stitching results in quilts easy enough for new quilters, but still fascinating for the experienced quilter. More experienced quilters will find new ways to tap into their creativity and beginners can expand their technical skills.

The techniques used to construct the *Streaks of Batiks* quilts are simple because only one fabric is used to form the center portion of the quilt. Most of the quilts are constructed of a main fabric and one or two border fabrics. The search for other fabrics for the quilt's borders and binding is automatically narrowed because the colors in the selected main fabric or batik suggest complementary colors for these areas. The quilts are quickly cut without templates or pinning and are economical because they generate very little wasted fabric.

Fabric Selection

Of utmost importance is the selection of the right streaked or striped fabric. Consider the end use of the quilt and the advantages and limitations of various color-streaked batiks and yarn-dyed or printed stripes. Select fabrics with a variety of colors and stripe widths and spacing for blocks with the greatest variety (Fig. 1, page 8).

Keep in mind that fabrics with evenly spaced stripes will yield less overall variety in the blocks and may be better suited to a tech-

OPPOSITE: BEACH BALLS, detail. Full quilt shown on page 76.

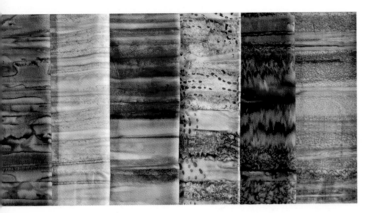

Fig. 1. Here are some examples of the many suitable fabrics available for this technique.

Fig. 2. These fabrics are not suitable for this technique because of their even repeats, direction, or spacing of the stripes.

Fig. 3. This length of hand-dyed fabric would make a stunning art quilt using the *Streaks of Batiks* technique.

nique that involves fussy cutting or stacking and aligning stripes using the Stack-n-Whack® technique. Avoid fabrics that are printed with a diagonal stripe (Fig. 2).

Fabrics with monochromatic color schemes or only subtle color variations often dictate use as a background fabric for silhouettes or appliqué. Bright multi-color batiks can create quilts that are very dramatic because the fabric does the work of providing drama and interest for the quilt. Appliquéd shapes and designs would compete for the viewer's eye with a background made from these bold fabrics.

A length of hand-dyed batik or streaked fabric can provide an exciting burst of color for a quilt constructed from blocks created with quarter-square triangles. The rich colors and striking contrasts are well suited to art quilts. The example of a hand-dyed fabric in Figure 3 is similar to one used to create a wallhanging with a feel of an Amish quilt using the traditional colors and feather quilting (Fig. 4).

There are several companies that produce striped batik fabrics and the stripes can run either horizontally (from selvage-to-selvage) or vertically (the length of the fabric or parallel to the selvage). See Figure 5 on page 10. Triangles cut from horizontally striped fabric are the easiest to arrange into blocks because color usually varies little across the stripe. The strips of fabric cut from these striped fabrics are limited to a double layer approximately 20" in length because you will cut the folded fabric from the selvages to the fold. Vertically striped fabrics often display many variations in color and color intensity. These variations can complicate the arrangement of the triangles into blocks, but will also form blocks that have the greatest variety of patterns and colors.

Fig. 4. ALMOST AMISH, 66" x 66". A hand-dyed fabric with traditional
Amish colors was used to create this quilt with the center block and feather
quilting motifs.

Fig. 5. These are examples of horizontally and vertically striped batiks on the bolts.

Square: 1 layer of fabric

fold

Strip: 4 layers of fabric

Fig. 6. The diagrams show a square of fabric cut diagonally and a strip of fabric cut into quarter-square triangles.

Triangles cut from square

Triangles cut from strip

Fig. 7. The direction of the stripes resulting from cutting a square and a strip are illustrated.

Quarter-Square Triangles from Strips Versus Squares

The *Streaks of Batiks* quilts are based on the use of strips to cut the quarter-square triangles instead of a square. The diagrams below show why strips are used rather than the square. It becomes obvious when using a striped or streaked batik that there are two distinct sets of quarter-square triangles created when the square is cut twice diagonally from corner to corner. The quarter-square triangles cut from a single square are made up of two triangles with the stripes or lines parallel to the base or hypotenuse of the triangles and two triangles with the stripes vertical to the base or running in the opposite direction.

For quilts made with the *Streaks of Batiks* technique, all quarter-square triangles should have stripes or designs that are parallel to the base of the triangle.

The second set of quarter-square triangles was cut from one four-layer strip. Note that all of the stripes are going in one direction and the stripes are horizontal to the base or hypotenuse of the triangles.

The quarter-square triangles used in the *Streaks of Batiks* technique are well suited to experimentation. This becomes obvious when reviewing the variety of quilts in this book. As a starting point, the author recommends that if you are not inclined to experiment that you start your journey with this technique by completing a quilt using the Quilt Master Plan directions that follow. All other quilts in this book are based upon these directions and techniques.

Fig. 8. SPECTRUM, 44" x 44". This is the author's first *Streaks of Batiks* quilt using one yard of a multi-colored vertically striped batik.

Streaks of Batiks Quilt Master Plan

Supply List

Fabrics

Please note that the technique used to create *Streaks of Batiks* quilts can be used to make lap quilts, wallhangings, table runners, or bed-size quilts. It is possible to create a wall quilt center with just a half yard of fabric or a queen-size quilt with multiple yards. Some quilters prefer to have established guidelines and insist on following a pattern with specific fabric requirements. For this reason, I will present the fabric requirements for an estimated 55" x 55" quilt. The block arrangement and borders will determine the actual size of the quilt. Experienced quilters are encouraged to experiment and create a quilt center or blocks for a border using this quarter-square triangle technique.

Yardage Requirements

Center of quilt: 1½ yards of a streaked batik, stripe, or linear print

Inner-accent border (optional): 2 yards

Outer border: 2 yards

Binding: Use either the accent border or outer border fabric for your binding fabric

Backing: A total of approximately three yards is needed for the backing of the quilt. Use leftover fabrics from the inner-accent border, outer borders, and body of the quilt to create an interesting pieced backing for the quilt. It may be necessary to add an additional solid fabric or one of the other fabrics in the quilt top to construct a suitably sized backing.

Batting: A piece of batting at least 6" longer and 4" wider than the quilt top

LEFT AND OPPOSITE DETAIL: SILK FLOWERS, 54" x 54". This is an example of a typical quilt that can be created with one fabric forming the whole center of the quilt.

Tools

Rotary cutter and mat

Acrylic rulers

24" x 8½", 24" x 6½", or 24" x 6"

90-degree triangle ruler with capacity to cut triangles up to 5½" or an acrylic ruler called a half- and quarter-square triangle ruler

8½" square ruler to trim blocks (optional)

Ruler to cut set-in triangles for blocks on-point (optional)

Design wall (optional): A flannel-backed plastic tablecloth or flannel sheet tacked to a wall or draped over a door can serve as a design wall.

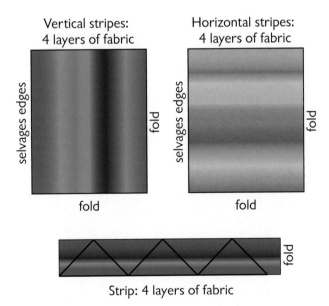

Fig. 1. Folding the fabric creates layers and allows 4 triangles to be cut at one time.

Cutting the Pieces

Note directions for folding fabric (*Streaks of Batiks* Cutting Techniques, pages 15–16) before cutting strips.

Quilt Size

Approximately 55" x 55" depending on block arrangement and border width

Block Size

7½"

Batik or Striped Fabric

Cut as many 4" strips as possible. Remember that stripes or streaks must run parallel to the long edge of the ruler.

Border Fabrics

Accent fabric: Cut 4 strips 2½" wide by the length of the fabric.

Outer borders: Cut 4 strips 6½" wide by the length of the fabric.

Binding

Cut 4 strips 2½" wide by the length of the fabric of either accent or outer border.

Backing

Single fabric or muslin quilt backs add little interest to the quilt. Use fabrics left over from the accent border, outer border, and the striped fabric for the center of the quilt to create a quilt backing. Even the ends cut from the first cut made to create the quarter-square triangles from the strips can be joined to form blocks, strips, or a grouping that can be used as part of the back of the quilt. Note that additional fabric may be necessary to complete a quilt backing at least 4" wider and 6" longer than the completed quilt top.

Streaks of Batiks Cutting Technique

The cutting technique used to make these quilts is based on the quarter-square triangle. Be aware that these quarter-square triangles are cut from strips and not squares of fabric because it is necessary to have the design or stripes of the triangles all running parallel to the base or hypotenuse of the quarter-square triangles (Fig. 1, page 14).

For fabrics with vertical stripes (stripes that run the length of the fabric), match selvages and fold the fabric in half lengthwise again matching the selvages. For fabrics with horizontal stripes (stripes that run across the fabric from selvage-to-selvage), align the stripes and selvages. It is not necessary to match the horizontal stripes of the top two and bottom two layers of fabric. Begin by removing the selvages using your rotary cutter and ruler by trimming ½" from the woven selvage edges. Next cut the strips with four layers at one time. Remember to always cut your strips with the stripes or streaks running parallel to the long edge of your ruler (Figs. 2 and 3).

Strips can be cut with widths of 2½" up to 5½". Do not vary the width of the strips within the quilt because the finished blocks will not result in units that are the same size or easily combined. The author prefers to cut strips 4" wide because the strips will yield a sufficient number of finished triangles for the finished blocks for the center of the quilt and allow for placement variations and styles. Avoid

Fig. 2. Ruler placement for cutting horizontal striped fabrics

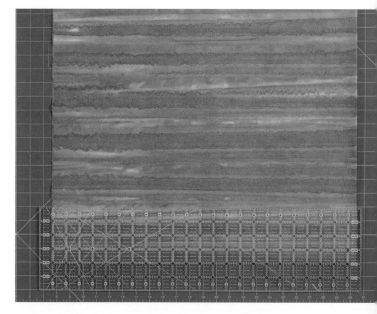

Fig. 3. Ruler placement for cutting vertical striped fabrics

stacking multiple layers after the strips have been cut because a slight variation in placement of each set of strips will cause a discrepancy in the points of the triangles.

Cut the quarter-square triangles by starting at the opposite end of the fold and placing the triangle ruler with the base of the triangle parallel to the bottom edge of the strip and along the ruler's printed line that designates the cut width of your strips (Fig. 4). Cut both sides of the triangle and this will result in one set of quarter-square triangles and one four-layer set of smaller triangles. Set these smaller sets of triangles aside for the backing or another project. Next, place the ruler with the base of the triangle on the top edge of the strip matching the diagonal line that resulted from the cutting of the previous set of triangles.

Repeat this process until you have cut as many triangles from the strip as possible. If there is not enough fabric to cut a full set of triangles near the fold of the strip, open the two remaining pieces of fabric (remember that you folded the fabric to create four layers of fabric) and cut two additional triangles by placing the line indicating the cut width of the strip at the base of the strips. If the base of your triangular ruler does not line up with the edge of the cut strip and the diagonal line of the previously cut triangle, it may be necessary to cut a new diagonal line by aligning the base of the triangular ruler with the cut edge of the two layers of the fabric strips.

Remember that accuracy and consistency in both cutting and stitching are important to create flat even-size blocks and avoid a quilt surface that resembles pyramids and waffles.

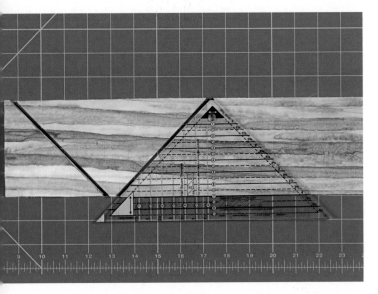

Fig. 4. Quarter-square triangles cut from one four-layer strip

Placement of Triangles

Use a flat surface or design wall to arrange the quarter-square triangles in units of four with the hypotenuse or long side of each triangle forming the outside of the block. Find a common element in each triangle and arrange them in four-triangle units or blocks.

Dark or light centers, similar color, shading, or location of a stripe can be elements that are used to select particular triangles to form units. When the fabric is folded in half either horizontally or vertically depending on the alignment of the stripes or pattern, four layers of fabric result. The top and bottom layers of the four layers are both from the same selvage edge, but the middle two layers are from the other selvage edge. Start with two sets of triangles cut from either the base of the strip or the top of the strip. Two sets of triangles from the top and bottom layers should form a block with matching elements and the two sets of triangles from the center two layers should form an additional block (Fig. 5). Note that many batik fabrics do not seem to have a right or wrong side and can be positioned on either side to create the most pleasing blocks.

Another technique to arrange the triangles into blocks involves separating all the triangles by some detail or element. For example, place all triangles with light centers in one pile and all triangles with a streak or strip at the base in another pile. Select and arrange four triangles for units that repeat a pattern or line. Keep in mind that not all triangles will join to form pleasing or cohesive blocks. These renegade triangles can be joined to form blocks and strips for the back of the quilt or a signature block (Fig. 6).

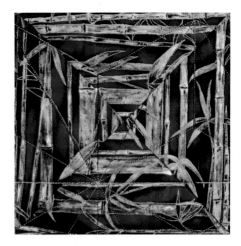

Fig. 5. Strips from the linear print of bamboo were cut into quarter-square triangles and combined to make blocks with matching design segments.

Fig. 6. Poorly matched blocks can be used as signature blocks or units on the back of the quilt.

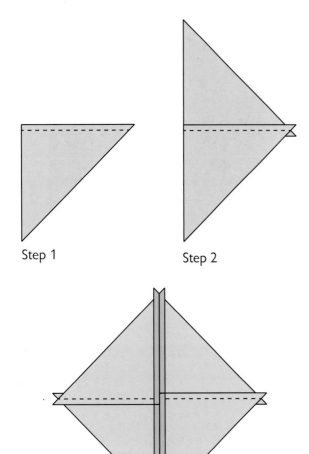

Step 1   Step 2

Step 3

Fig. 7. Block construction

Fig. 8. Completed block ready for trimming

Constructing the Blocks

Step 1: For each four-triangle unit, pin one side of each of the pairs of two triangles together. Stitch these units together using a ¼" seam allowance (Fig. 7).

> **Important note:** A generous seam allowance and the thread from a stitched seam can reduce the block's dimensions. Use a scant ¼" seam allowance when stitching the triangles and half blocks together. This will result in finished blocks measuring approximately 7½" square.

Step 2: Press the seams of the two units in opposite directions and pin each half of the block together matching the center seam and edges. Stitch again using a ¼" seam allowance (Fig. 7).

Step 3: Press this seam open (Figs. 7 and 8).

Trim all blocks to the same size using an acrylic square ruler with a line running diagonally from corner to corner (Fig. 9, page 19).

Measure the smallest block and trim all other blocks to the same size. Place the square ruler with the diagonal line on opposite corners of the block along the seam line before trimming. Check to make certain that the diagonal line passes through the center of the block where the triangles meet (Fig. 10, page 19).

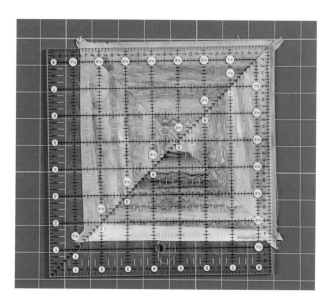

Fig. 9. Square up blocks using a ruler with a diagonal line that runs from corner to corner and through the center of the acrylic ruler.

Fig. 10. All seams should meet at the corners of the trimmed blocks. Note the poorly aligned corner seams of the trimmed lavender block.

Arranging the Blocks

It is easiest to use a design wall or large flat surface to choose the most pleasing arrangement for the blocks. With many types of fabrics there will be light, medium, and dark blocks. Place the blocks in piles of light, medium, and dark. Experiment by placing the light blocks in the center and surround them with medium blocks. Use the darker blocks for a frame. Blocks can be lined up in rows or placed on-point. Match the side of the blocks with similar intensity and design with those of their neighbors (Fig. 11). This arrangement will create a square unit that appears to be part of the quilt artist's vision and emerge as a well-planned pattern.

The fabric used for LEX'S GARDEN has bands of streaked color that flowed from almost white to a light

Fig. 11. Notice the blending of colors of the adjacent blocks.

Fig. 12. This commercially printed piece of fabric is similar to the fabric used to create the background for LEX'S GARDEN. Note the bands of color and varying visual textures.

Fig. 13. LEX'S GARDEN, detail. Full quilt on page 40. Observe the placement of the blocks created from these different strata of color.

green to a blue (Fig. 12). Observe the placement of the blocks created from these different strata of color. The deeper blue was used for the sky and the lighter green blocks were placed in the foreground. The blocks in the medium-color range were placed in the middle behind the fence and the gardener. A piece of fabric with a bright flower print was inserted behind the fence to simulate a flower patch (Fig. 13).

Some fabrics create blocks that seem to have a life of their own and are better dealt with as separate units. Sashing between the blocks treats them as separate units allowing the quilter to join contrasting blocks and gives the eye a place to rest. Wide sashing tends to separate the blocks and narrower sashing enables the quilter to join the blocks with a minimal amount of visual interruption. Sashing can be used between rows or with blocks on-point, but blocks on-point will also require set-in triangles to be added to the outer edges and half-square triangles to be added to the corners of each end.

Special Consideration When Setting Blocks On-Point

When creating quilts with blocks set on-point, the author prefers to attach borders with a ¼" space between the points of the blocks on-point and the border strips. After machine quilting, points often lose their definition when the borders are placed at the point of each block. Allow an extra ½" to 1" on each set-in triangle and end triangle so that the sides of the center of the quilt can be trimmed placing a ruler ½" from the points of the outside ends of blocks set on-point (Fig. 14).

Fig. 14. FIREFLY, 54" x 54". Note that the same fabric is used for the sashing, set-in triangles, and one of the border fabrics.

Fig. 15. SILK FLOWERS, detail. The outer and inner borders of the quilt were chosen based on the dominant colors in the batik used to create the whole center of this quilt.

Fig. 16. The fabric color for the narrow framed border of this quilt also appears in the blocks created from this hand-dyed fabric.

Choosing Borders for the Quilt Blocks

Borders allow you to frame and contain your design (Fig. 15). Sometimes you will find the seemingly perfect border fabric with all of the colors of your original striped fabric or one with the special color that you would like to emphasize, but when you place it next to your constructed blocks, it gets lost or appears uninteresting. This is where a solid color or fabric that reads solid can create a transition. Experience and experimentation has shown that often a 2" strip of fabric is just what is needed to create a place for the eye to rest and frame the blocks. Audition fabrics for the borders by folding and stacking the fabrics on the design wall next to the quilt center. Sometimes the perfect color for the inside border is hinted at in the original striped fabric (Fig. 16). Two solid colors can also be used to create the inner borders. One color may look better next to a printed outer border, but not be as pleasing when placed next to the completed blocks. Try two different colors that complement each other and join them to form the inner borders. Again, audition your choices before cutting and sewing on the strips. Do not add unnecessary borders as this will suggest that you did not have enough fabric to enlarge the center of your quilt and you are trying to stretch the quilt with multiple borders that appear too wide for the quilt.

Quilt Back

Construct the back of the quilt using extra blocks and scraps from the front of the quilt, the accent, and border fabrics. The backing should be at least 4" wider and 6" longer than the top. The majority of the seams should run vertically as this will minimize stretching of the fabrics.

Pieces of fabric placed with the lengthwise grain of the fabric running the length of the quilt back will also have less stretch than those on the crosswise grain of the fabric. Use a layout similar to the one described on page 31 (FIREFLY, quilt backing) to construct a backing for the quilt, or use your imagination and remnants of the fabrics used for the front of the quilt to make an interesting design for the back of the quilt (Figs. 17a–d).

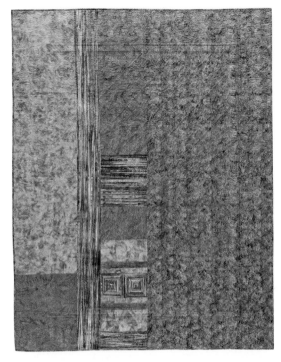

Fig. 17c. FUSION, back. Quilt shown on page 77.

Fig. 17a. SWIRLS, back. Quilt shown on page 78.

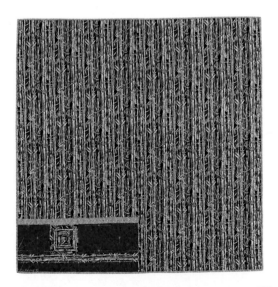

Fig. 17d. BAMBOOZLED, back. Quilt shown on page 78. The back of BAMBOOZLED contains a strip of fabric left over from the borders and one block. This area can be used for the artist's signature or dedication.

Fig. 17b. BEACH BALLS, back. Quilt shown on page 76.

Fig. 18. The continuous-line pantograph of hearts and swirls complement the colors of this pink and lavender batik.

BELOW: Fig. 19. Corner and set-in triangles of plain or solid color fabrics provide a showcase for detailed or feather quilting.

Quilting

With this technique and the selection of a striped fabric, the resulting quilt often creates a design where elaborate machine quilting would be lost on the quilt top. The home quilter might consider a stitch-in-the-ditch technique or machine or hand quilt the finished piece. Another option would be to employ a longarm quilter to use a pantograph to add subtle texture to the surface. When selecting a pattern for a pantograph, keep in mind the feel, the theme of the fabrics used, scale of the design, and whether you would like to add texture and interest or a distinct design (Fig. 18). Avoid designs that have multiple stitching lines in one location because these heavily stitched areas have a tendency to recede or pop up on the surface of the quilt. Wide solid-color sashing or set-in triangles allow for more creativity (Fig. 19). Bold thread color selection and design choices in these areas can add interest to the quilt. Neutral or monochromatic colored stripes can provide a texture background for appliqué, thread painting, and surface embellishments.

Finishing the Quilt

Add the binding and a sleeve for any quilt that will be hung or displayed on a wall. Join the 2½" binding strips with a horizontal seam. Press the wrong sides of the joined binding strips in half, matching the two long cut edges. Create a sleeve for the quilt if you intend to hang the quilt on a wall. The raw edges of the sleeve should be positioned at the top back of the quilt before the binding is sewn to the sides of the quilt. Attach the binding to the front of the quilt with a ¼" seam allowance. Hand stitch the folded edge of the binding to the back of the quilt, just covering the line of stitching that resulted from applying the binding to the front of the quilt. Attach any trims, buttons, or beads that you would like to use for embellishment (Fig. 20). The quilt is not complete without a signature or label.

BELOW: SILK FLOWERS, 54" x 54". Quilt shown on page 12. This is a typical arrangement using the *Streaks of Batiks* Quilt Master Plan.

Fig. 20. GRAZING SEA TURTLES has individually attached seagrass blades, a vintage sterling silver sea horse pin, beads, shells, coral, and sea glass.

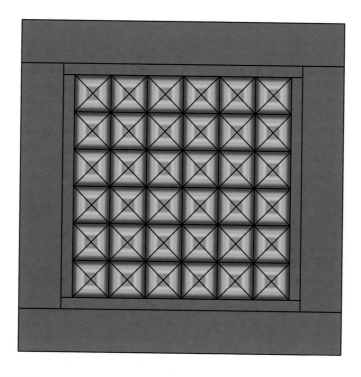

Words from Experience

▼ Save the triangular piece of fabric from the first cut made on each strip. These pieces can be used for combining units to incorporate into the back of the quilt.

▼ Set aside the pieces that remain near the fold after cutting all of the quarter-square triangles from the strips. These can also be used to create an interesting backing for the quilt or be combined with other scraps to create a triangle needed to complete a block.

▼ Batik fabrics have an advantage when combining triangles to form blocks because it is usually possible to use either side of a batik fabric. This enables one to better combine the triangles to match a particular color, shading, or stripe.

▼ A half-square and quarter-square triangle ruler is useful in cutting the quarter-square triangles from the strips because the width of the triangle is printed on the ruler and this line should be placed along the cut edge of the strips. The ruler also has a shaded triangular area at the tip. The base of this shaded triangle should be placed along the top edge of the strip and creates a 90-degree corner with a blunt end or cut-off point. It is easier to sew a blunt or straight edge than a pointed unit. The fabric is less likely to be pushed down into the bed of the sewing machine by the needle.

▼ There are rulers on the market that are designed to cut set-in triangles. Many half-square and quarter-triangle rulers are too small to accomplish the task of cutting larger set-in triangular units. The author recommends calculating the width of the strips to cut the set-in triangle units by taking the measurement of one side of the unfinished blocks and then deducting 1½". These calculations will give you the width of the strip needed to cut these triangles and allow for the seam allowance and a little extra for the ¼" space between the blocks and the borders after trimming. Remember that the long edge of the set-in triangle should be on the straight grain of the fabric and not the bias. If the blocks are joined with sashing, the finished width of the sashing must be added to the measurement of the side of the block when calculating the width of the strips for the set-in triangles.

▼ A design wall gives the quilt artist an entirely different view of a work in progress. Being able to stand back from a quilt that is in progress allows the artist to more easily see the distribution of color and other elements. The design wall does not have to be elaborate or permanent. A piece of flannel draped over a door or curtain rod or a flannel-backed plastic tablecloth will provide a surface to position triangles, blocks, and borders without pins or tape.

LEFT: SILK FLOWER, detail. Full quilt shown on page 12.
OPPOSITE: HEART BEAT, detail. Full quilt shown on page 28.

Quilts

HEART BEAT 28

IRIS 32

RIVER BED 36

LEX'S GARDEN 40

GRAZING TURTLES 48

ORNAMENTATION 56

HEART BEAT, 55¼" x 55¼". Made by the author.

HEART BEAT

Finished quilt: 55¼" x 55¼"

Direction of fabric streaks: Horizontal

Trimmed block size: 7¼"

Finished block size: 6¾"

Number of blocks: 25

Block arrangement: 5 blocks by 5 blocks

Supplies

1½ yards of a horizontal striped or streaked
   fabric

1 yard of first inner-border fabric and binding

¼ yard second inner-border fabric

1¾ yards outer border fabric

2¾ yards backing fabric

60" x 62" piece of batting

Cut

Follow the directions for folding and cutting
horizontal stripes.

Horizontal Stripe

▼ 12 to 13 strips 4" wide cut selvage-to-
   selvage. Cut as many as possible.

▼ You will be cutting 2 strips at the same time
   from the folded fabric.

▼ Cut strips into quarter-square triangles with
   a quarter-square triangle ruler.

First Inner Border and Binding Fabric

▼ First inner border: 4 strips 2½" wide cut
   selvage-to-selvage

▼ Binding: 6 strips 2½" wide cut selvage-to-
   selvage

Second Inner-border Fabric

▼ 4 strips 1¼" wide cut selvage-to-selvage

Outer Border

▼ 4 strips 8½" wide cut parallel to the selvages
   or the length of the fabric

Directions

Follow the directions for constructing the blocks under the Master Plan. Trim all blocks to a uniform size. Using a design wall, combine completed blocks matching shading, color, or intensity of color to form a pleasing arrangement. Join rows of blocks using a ¼" seam allowance. Press the rows of blocks in opposite directions and join the rows. Add the three border fabrics by starting with the first inner border, adding the narrow second inner border, and finally attaching the wider outer border (Fig. 1).

Backing

Trim selvages and cut one length of fabric 62" long. The remaining approximate 36" of the fabric is to be cut lengthwise down the fold. Join the two 20" wide pieces of fabric with a strip of the horizontally striped or streaked fabric or a combination of left-over pieces from the quilt top. Stitch the two pieces of fabric (40" x 62" and 20" x 72") together along the length of the two pieces. The constructed narrow panel will be longer than the 62" piece that you first cut. Trim the narrower panel of joined fabrics the same length as the larger width piece of fabric (Fig. 2, page 31). Save the extra piece of fabric to construct a label or use as part of a matching pillow.

Finished sizes:

Block: 6¾"

Inner border: 2"

Second border: ¾"

Outer border: 8"

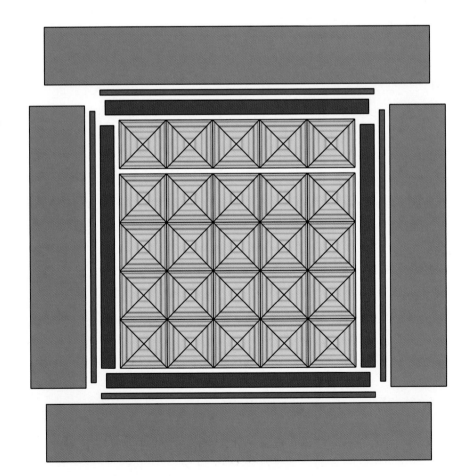

Fig. 1. Block and border layout for HEART BEAT

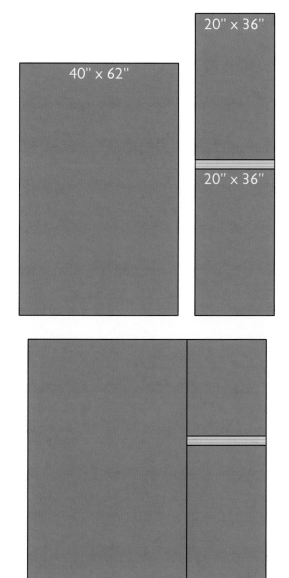

Fig. 2. A simple quilt back can be created from a length of fabric and an insert of the original striped batik or fabrics left over from the construction of the quilt front.

Another option is to be creative and construct a quilt backing with leftover scraps of fabric. Join the first cut pieces from the cutting of the quarter-square triangular pieces and any extra blocks, strips, or triangles. Leftover border fabrics can also be included.

The backs of quilts are areas that can be used to experiment and use not only leftover blocks or sample blocks, but those blocks that had triangles that were not as well matched as those used on the front of the quilt. The author refers to these types of blocks as mismatched or "renegade" blocks. Four leftover blocks, strips of the sashing fabric, and the excess fabric from cutting the strips for the quarter-square triangles were combined in the back of the quilt called FIREFLY (Fig. 3). This not only adds an element of design, but interest to the back of the quilt.

Fig. 3. FIREFLY, back. Quilt shown on page 21. The use of leftover fabric adds interest to the back of this quilt.

IRIS, 42" x 49½". Made by the author.

IRIS

Finished quilt: 42" x 49½"
Direction of fabric streaks: Vertical
Trimmed block size: 6½"
Finished block size: 6"
Number of blocks: 12
Block arrangement: 3 blocks x 4 blocks

Supplies

⅝ yard of a vertical striped or streaked fabric
1 yard sashing and second-border fabric
¼ yard inner-border fabric
1½ yards outer-border fabric and binding
2½ yards backing fabric
46" x 56" piece of batting

Cut

Follow directions for folding and cutting a vertical striped or streaked fabric on page 15. Remember to always place the ruler parallel to the stripe when cutting strips.

Main Fabric

▼ Vertical striped or streaked batik
▼ 11 strips 3½" wide cut parallel to the selvage

▼ You may have to open the folded fabric to cut the last strip.
▼ Cut all strips into quarter-square triangles by placing the quarter-square triangle's 3½" designated line along the cut edge of the strips.

Sashing and Second-Border Fabric

▼ 11 strips 2" wide cut selvage-to-selvage
▼ Cut 3 of these strips into 15 sashing pieces, 2" x 6½".
▼ 4 strips will be used for sashing on outside edges and between columns.
▼ 4 strips will be used for the second outer border.

Inner-Border Fabric

▼ 4 strips 1½" wide cut selvage-to-selvage

Outer-Border and Binding Fabric

▼ **Outer Border:** 4 strips 7" wide cut parallel to the selvages
▼ **Binding:** 4 strips 2½" wide cut parallel to the selvages

Backing Fabric

▼ 1 piece 56" by the width of fabric
▼ 1 piece 30" by the width of fabric, cut again along the fold to make 2 pieces, 20" x 30"

Directions

Follow the directions for arranging triangles and constructing blocks on pages 16–18. Trim all blocks to a uniform size of 6½". Using a design wall, place the blocks in a pleasing arrangement of three columns of four blocks each. On the bottom side of each block, stitch a sashing piece (2" x 6½") and add the sashing pieces to the top of each of the blocks in the top row. Insert the sashing strips between the columns of blocks and on the two outer sides. Add the narrow inner border and matching sashing-fabric border before adding the final outer border.

Be creative and design your own quilt backing or use the cutting directions to construct the quilt backing. Join the two 20" wide pieces of fabric along their width using a narrow strip of leftover streaked fabric or any border fabric. The cut width of this strip used to join the two 20" wide pieces should be at least 2" to avoid a ridge from multiple seams. Using a ¼" seam allowance, sew the narrower joined fabric panel to the piece cut 56" in length by sewing along one long side. Trim the narrow panel to the same length as the wider piece of fabric. Press the seam to one side.

Layer the quilt top, batting, and backing. Select an appropriate pattern or design for the quilting. Keep in mind that the sashing strips are a suitable area for stitch-in-the-ditch quilting. Apply the binding and be certain to include a signature or label.

The layout for the block arrangement and borders for IRIS is shown.

Finished sizes:

Block: 6"

Sashing: 1½"

Inner border: 1"

Second border: 1½"

Outer border: 6½"

RIVER BED, 61½" x 61½". Made by the author.

RIVER BED

Finished quilt: 61½" × 61½"

Direction of fabric streaks: Vertical

Trimmed block size: 8"

Finished block size: 7½"

Number of blocks: 25

Block arrangement: Set on-point: 4 blocks over 3 blocks, 4 blocks over 3 blocks, 4 blocks over 3 blocks, 4 blocks

Supplies

2 yards of a vertical striped or streaked batik fabric

⅝ yard inner-border fabric

1 yard for set-in triangles and corner triangles

2 yards outer-border fabric

⅝ yard for binding

3 yards backing fabric

64" × 66" piece of batting

Cut

Follow directions for folding and cutting a vertical streaked or striped fabric on pages 15–16.

Note that the base of the ruler should always be placed parallel to the fabric's stripe, streak, or linear print.

Main Fabric

▼ Vertical striped, streaked batik, or linear print

▼ 8 strips 4½" wide cut parallel to the selvage

▼ Remember to fold the fabric in half and match the selvages. You will be cutting four layers or two strips at the same time. Cut strips into quarter-square triangles using the quarter-square triangle ruler by placing the 4½" line for quarter-square triangles along the cut edge of the strips.

Inner-Border Fabric

▼ 6 strips 2" wide cut selvage-to-selvage

Set-in Triangles and Corner Triangles

▼ Cut 6 strips 6½" wide cut from the length of the fabric and parallel to the selvage. Note that you are cutting two strips at one time.

▼ Cut 12 quarter-square triangles from these strips to use as set-in triangles on the outside edges of the blocks.

▼ Cut 2 squares 6½" × 6½" and cut these squares once diagonally from corner-to-corner to form 4 half-square triangles (Fig. 1, page 38).

6½" square

Fig. 1. The four corner units are cut from squares to form half-square triangles.

Outer-border Fabric

▼ 4 strips 8½" cut the length of the fabric (parallel to the selvage)

Binding

▼ 7 strips 2½" cut selvage-to-selvage

Backing

▼ 1 piece 40" x 72"

▼ 1 piece 40" x 36" cut in half lengthwise along the 36" fold

▼ Note that this will create a backing about 6" larger than necessary, but the simple measurements, ease of cutting, and a minimal number of seams are a time-saver.

Directions

Follow the directions on pages 16–18 for arranging and constructing the blocks from four quarter-square triangles. Trim all blocks to a uniform size (8" in the example). Using a design wall, arrange the blocks as shown in figure 2 on page 39. Along the outer edges insert the set-in quarter square triangles. Stitch the blocks together in diagonal rows using a ¼" seam allowance and press the seams of each diagonal row in opposite directions. Join the rows diagonally and press the seams in one direction.

Place the half-square corner triangles at the four corners of the outer blocks at the top and bottom, but first fold the half-square triangles in half and finger press a line to indicate the center of the long bias edge of the triangle. Match the center of the half-square triangle to the center of the side of the blocks on-point at each corner. Stitch with a ¼" seam allowance being careful not to stretch the bias edge of the half-square triangle. The straight grain of the triangles should be on the outer edges of the set-in triangles and the two outside edges of each corner triangle (Fig. 2, page 39).

With a long acrylic ruler, trim the edges of the center of the quilt top by placing the ½" line parallel to the outside corner of the four-block rows. This will provide ample seam fabric for a ¼" seam allowance to join the inner-border strips and an additional ¼" that allows the center section to appear to float on the background. The extra ¼" also eliminates the lost points of these blocks when the inner border is added and the surface shrinks after quilting. Add the inner and outer borders.

The back of the quilt can be made from a two-yard length of fabric and a joined panel constructed from two pieces of fabric cut from half of the width of the remaining one yard of fabric. A narrow strip, created by joining leftover shapes and pieces of fabric and inserted between the two pieces of fabric for the panel, will provide an interesting design element for the back of the quilt and will also give purpose to the seam construction.

Construct the backing for the quilt and layer the quilt top, batting, and backing. Select a quilting design or pattern that suits the theme of the quilt and machine or hand quilt the layers together. Apply the binding and create your own label.

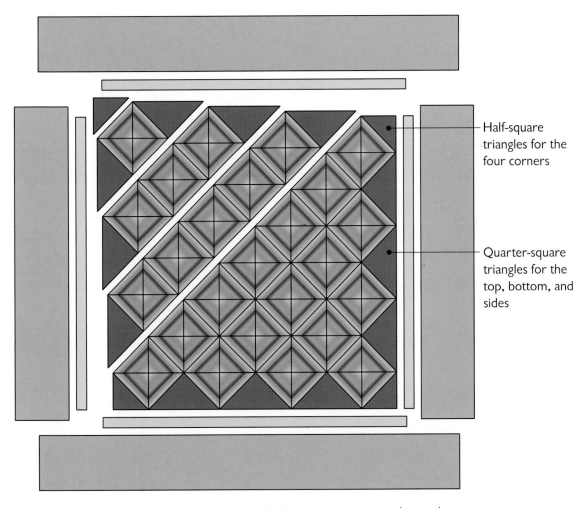

Half-square triangles for the four corners

Quarter-square triangles for the top, bottom, and sides

Fig. 2. The diagram shows the diagonal block setting, set-in triangles, and borders of RIVER BED.

Finished sizes:
Block: 7½"
Inner border: 1½"
Outer border: 8"

LEX'S GARDEN, 56½" x 56½". Made by the author.

LEX'S GARDEN

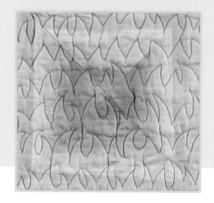

Finished quilt: 56½" x 56½"
Direction of fabric streaks: Horizontal
Trimmed block size: 7"
Finished block size: 6½"
Number of blocks: 25
Block arrangement: 5 blocks by 5 blocks

Supplies

1½ yards of a horizontal striped or streaked fabric

½ yard inner-border fabric—additional fabric may be necessary if this fabric is to be used for the binding and/or part of the backing for the quilt.

3¼ yards border, girl's dress, binding, and part of backing fabric

Additional backing fabric to equal approximately a total of 3¼ yards

½ yard wood-grained or white fence fabric

⅛ yard floral print for the flower garden

61" x 63" piece of batting

Additional Fabrics

Hat: straw or textured print

Hands and face: flesh color

Dress sleeves: print or color to coordinate with dress fabric

Dress yoke and collar: coordinate with dress fabric

Shoes: black or brown

Basket, flowers, and leaves: suitable prints

Cat: fur or textured print

Cat's collar and heart tag: red and suitable color or print for collar

Bird (including wings and beak): feather or textured print

Cat and bird eyes: printed fabric with small detailed circles

Cut

▼ **Background for appliqué:** 4" strips cut into quarter-square triangles

▼ **Inner border:** 4 strips 2½" wide cut the width of the fabric

▼ **Outer border:** 4 strips 10½" wide cut the length of the fabric

▼ **Binding:** 6 strips 2½" wide cut the width of the fabric

▼ **Fence:** 7 pieces 5" x 11½"

▼ **Rails:** 2 pieces 16" x 2"
        2 pieces 3" x 2"

Directions

Follow the directions on pages 16–18 for arranging and constructing the blocks. Trim all blocks to a uniform size. Using a design wall, combine the completed blocks to create a background for the appliqué figures and fence. Arrange the blocks to create an illusion of a sky and foreground (Fig. 1). Odd or "renegade" blocks can be positioned in the area that will be covered by the garden, fence, and figures. Sew the blocks together in rows and then join the rows. Prepare the appliqué pieces to be applied using your preferred technique with freezer paper, fusible web,

or other method. Note the suggestions regarding the preparation of the fence rails and posts on pages 44–45.

Position and stitch the garden fabric to the background before applying the fence rails and posts. Use the photograph of the quilt as a guide in arranging the garden, fence, and other appliqués or create your own arrangement of this young girl with her cat and bird in the garden (Fig. 2, page 43).

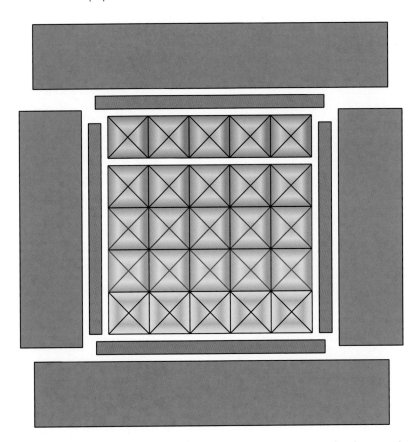

Fig. 1. LEX'S GARDEN: The block arrangement serves as a background for the appliqué and the two borders frame the design.

Finished sizes:

Block: 6½"

Inner border: 2"

Outer border: 10"

Apply the girl, cat, and bird appliqué pieces (pages 46–47) to the quilt center after the garden fabric and fence rails and posts have been stitched. This can be done by hand or machine depending on your preferred appliqué technique. Stitch the pieces in layers with the bottommost pieces applied first. For example, the cat's left ear and body were applied before the right ear and collar.

Stitch the inner border and the wider outer border to the center of the quilt. Construct the quilt backing using extra fabrics from the quarter-square triangle blocks, borders, and appliqué pieces or choose a simple seamed backing for this quilt.

Layer the quilt top, batting, and backing. Choose a quilting pattern that will enhance the design of the quilt. Echo quilting is often used to outline appliquéd shapes and figures. Detail can be added to the figures with different patterns of stitching to simulate feathers on the bird, wood grain on the fence posts, fur on the cat, and folds in the sleeves and dress. Apply the binding and consider attaching a sleeve for hanging if you anticipate the quilt being used as a wallhanging. A separate fabric sleeve can be included with the quilt if it is a gift and you are uncertain of the intended end use of this quilt. Instructions can be included for attaching the sleeve and it can be sewn to the back of this quilt at a later date. Be sure to sign and date this quilt so that future generations will know who made it and when it was made. The pattern for the watering can appliqué can be used as a label.

Fig. 2. The cat and bird give the design a visual balance when combined with the female figure in the hat and long dress.

Fence and Rail Construction

Note that the rails and fence posts are a double thickness so that the background and seams from the blocks beneath them are not evident when the rails and posts are applied to the background fabric. The double thickness and no raw edges on both make it possible to stitch the rails and posts in position with a machine straight or buttonhole stitch.

To form the rails for the fence, fold the four rectangles (16" by 2" and 3" by 2") in half lengthwise with the wrong side of the fabric together and stitch a ¼" seam allowance. On an ironing board, center the seam allowance in the middle of one side of the fabric tube and press the seam open (Fig. 3). It is not necessary to finish the ends of the rails because they will be concealed in the border seam or covered by the fence posts.

The fence posts are formed by folding the 5" by 11½" strips (Step 1) in half lengthwise with the right sides of the fabric together to form a piece 2½" by 11½". Make a line of stitching ¼" across one end of the strip (Step 2). Trim the top seam allowance corner near the fold. Finger press the seam open and turn the strip right-side out. Center this short seam in the center of the top portion of the strip and press. The point for the fence post has now been formed (Step 3). Fold the strip in half with the wrong sides of the fabric together, matching the raw edge sides and bottom edges. The bottom edges of the fabric that now form a facing for the point of the fence post should also match. Make a ¼" line of stitching that runs from the edge of the facing to the base of the strip (Step 4). On the ironing board, center the seam in the middle of the fence post and press the seam open (Step 5). Turn up the bottom raw edge of the strip approximately ¼" and press firmly in place. Repeat for the remaining fence posts (Fig. 4, page 45).

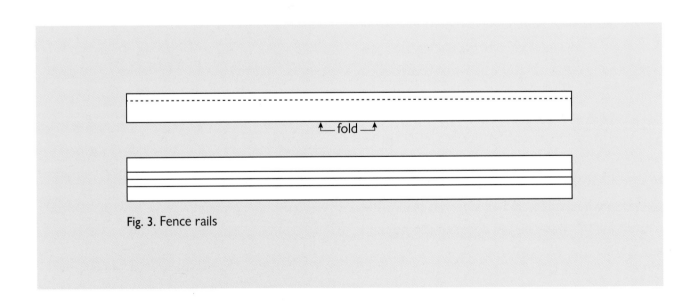

Fig. 3. Fence rails

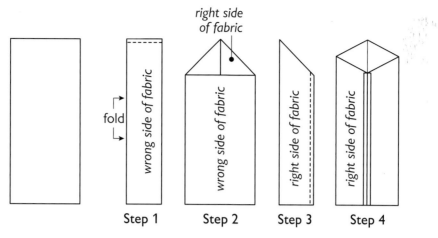

Fig. 4. Fence posts are easily created from rectangular pieces of fabric.

Embellishments

If the intended purpose of the quilt is a wall-hanging and it is not to be used by a young child, this quilt can be a canvas for many different types of embellishments. Beads, pearls, and buttons could adorn the dress and hat. Vintage floral pins might provide an added dimension to the flower basket or garden. Three-dimensional fabric flowers would add detail and texture to the garden, flower basket, or hat. Clusters of dimensional flowers or shapes created using the Japanese origami folded-fabric technique could form a hatband or trim.

There are many patterns and templates for the creation of three-dimensional flowers or accents. The flower resembling a mum blossom on the girl's hat was made using a plastic circular ruching template to mark the zigzag lines for a running stitch to gather the fabric and adjust the size of the blossom. There are also two-part plastic templates available that form consistently sized gathered circles called yo-yos which can form flowers, clusters of blossoms, or flower centers to add dimension to the surface of the quilt. The possibilities are endless.

LEX'S GARDEN, girl
Enlarge 400%

LEX'S GARDEN, bird
Shown at 100%

LEX'S GARDEN, watering can
Enlarge 200%

LEX'S GARDEN, cat
Enlarge 200%

GRAZING TURTLES, 58½" x 58½". Made by the author.

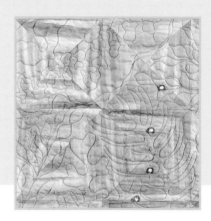

GRAZING TURTLES

Finished quilt: 58½" × 58½"

Direction of fabric streaks: Vertical

Trimmed block size: 6½"

Finished block size: 6"

Number of blocks: 36

Block arrangement: 6 blocks by 6 blocks

Supplies

1½ yards streaked fabric

⅓ yard inner-border fabric

2 yards outer-border fabric

3 yards backing fabric or remnants equaling
   this yardage

½ yard binding fabric

⅔ yard seagrass fabric

1⅓ yards lightweight fusible interfacing

Turtle eyes: scraps of small circular or swirl
   print

Turtle shells: suitable print or batik with
   segments or blocks

Turtle legs: textured print

63" × 66" piece of batting

Batting scraps to add more dimension to the
   turtles' shells (optional)

Assorted beads, pearls, glass, and coral for
   embellishment

Cut

▼ **Background for appliqué:** 3½" strips, cut
   into quarter-square triangles

▼ **Inner border:** 4 strips 2½" wide cut the
   width of the fabric

▼ **Outer border:** 4 strips 10" wide cut the
   length of the fabric or parallel to the
   selvages

▼ **Binding:** 6 strips 2½" wide cut the width of
   the fabric

Directions

Follow the directions on pages 16–18 for arranging and constructing the blocks. Trim all blocks to a uniform size. Using a design wall, combine the completed blocks to create a background for the appliquéd turtles, seagrass, and other embellishments. The turtles and seagrass will cover some blocks and mismatched blocks can be placed to form the bottom row of the background piece. Sew the blocks together in rows and then join the rows (Fig. 1, page 50). Prepare the appliqué pieces to be applied using your preferred technique employing freezer paper, fusible web, or other materials and methods. Note the suggestions for preparing the seagrass for attaching to the finished quilt background.

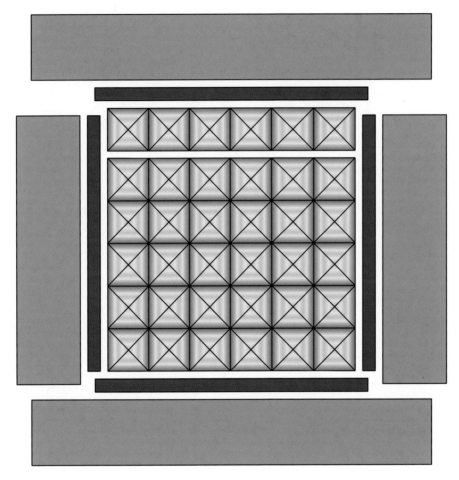

Fig. 1. The neutral-colored blocks make a background for the underwater display of turtles and seagrass in GRAZING TURTLES.

Finished sizes

Block: 6"

Inner border: 2"

Outer border: 9½"

Turtles

Using your preferred technique for appliqué, prepare the turtle pieces (pages 53–54). Arrange the turtles on the constructed background and pin or baste in place. It is possible to add dimension to the turtles by cutting leftover pieces of light to medium-weight batting pieces slightly smaller than the turtles' shells and heads. Insert these pieces of batting beneath the appliqué pieces for the tur-

tles before they are stitched to the background. Appliqué the pieces in place with an appliqué stitch and matching thread. The eyes of the turtles are formed by cutting circles about the size of a quarter, making running stitches a scant ¼" inside the cut edge, pulling the thread to gather the circles and flattening the disk to form a round circle. Decrease or increase the size of the cut circles to achieve the desired size of each eye.

Attach the inner border and wider outer border. Prepare the quilt back and layer the top, batting, and backing. Plan the quilting design keeping in mind that the lower edge of the center of the quilt will be covered with seagrass and possibly other embellishments. The pictured example of GRAZING TURTLES is machine quilted in a freehand design incorporating underwater vegetation motifs. It is desirable to select designs that have the same intensity of stitching to avoid areas that recede or pop out on the surface of the finished quilt. Add a sleeve for hanging and bind the quilt before the seagrass blades are attached and other embellishments added.

Seagrass

Trace between 28 and 35 blades of grass (page 55) onto the paper side of fusible interfacing, varying the length of the blades between 9" to 3" in length. Cut on the traced line for each blade of grass and fuse the interfacing to the wrong side of the grass fabric with the base of each blade along a cut edge and leaving approximately ½" between each blade.

With the right sides of the fabrics together, pin a second piece of grass fabric to the piece with the fused grass blades. Starting at the bottom of each blade, backstitch and stitch along the edge of the interfacing to form the blades. Backstitch again at the base leaving the bottom edge open. Stitch all of the blades before you cut them apart as it is easier to maneuver a larger piece of fabric than narrow strips.

Trim each blade leaving a ¼" or less seam allowance. Clip the curves at the top of each blade

and turn the blades right-side out with the aid of a wooden chopstick. Roll the edges between your fingers as you press the sides of the blades. All of the borders should be applied to the constructed center panel with the turtle appliqués. The quilt should be quilted and bound before the seagrass, shells, pearls, coral, and other embellishments are added.

Alternating lengths of seagrass blades should be arranged along the bottom edge of the background fabric with the base of each blade extending approximately ¼" beyond the background and over the inner-border seam. Fold the base of each blade under about ¼" and hand sew the blade bases securely to the quilt, avoiding a messy collection of stitches and threads on the back of the quilt. Twist, turn, and slant each blade until you have a pleasing arrangement. Pin the blades in place, and with matching thread, tack each blade to the background fabric in several locations. Work with the quilt on a flat surface so that the quilt will hang flat and the grass does not pull at the background fabric. Secure the shells, beads, and other embellishments with the thread that matches the background fabric.

Fig. 2. The seagrass and other embellishments were added after the whole quilt had been quilted and bound.

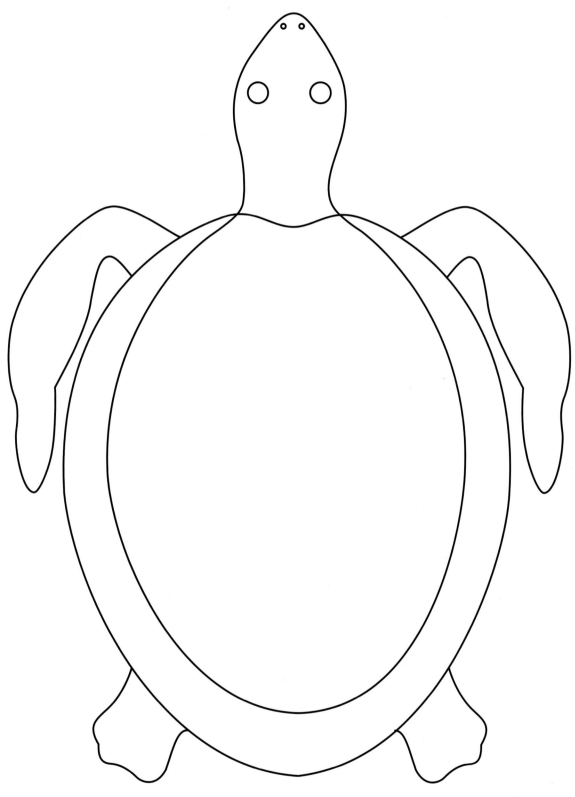

GRAZING TURTLES, turtle 1
Enlarge 200%

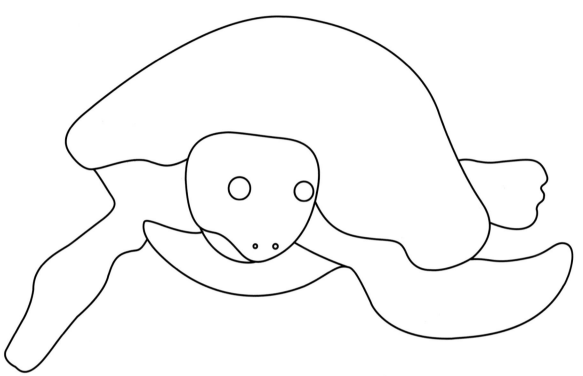

GRAZING TURTLES, turtle 2
Enlarge 200%

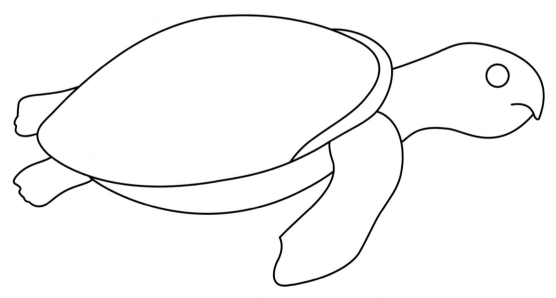

GRAZING TURTLES, turtle 3
Enlarge 200%

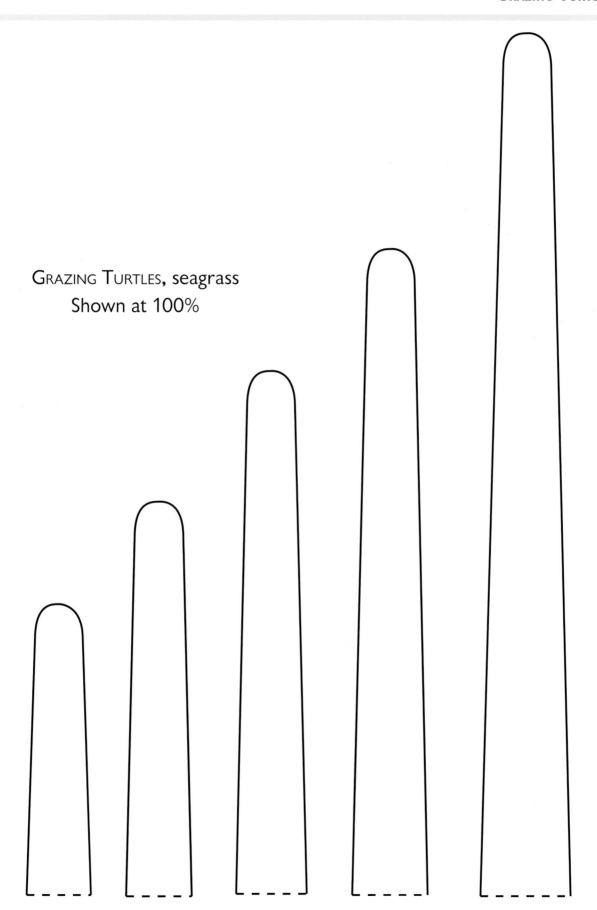

GRAZING TURTLES, seagrass
Shown at 100%

ORNAMENTATION, 65" x 65". Made by the author.

ORNAMENTATION

Finished quilt: 65" x 65"

Direction of fabric streaks: Horizontal

Ornament block size: 9½" finished

Trimmed border block size: 7"

Finished border block size: 6½"

Number of ornament blocks: 16

Number of border blocks: 32

Seminole Patchwork Christmas Ornaments

The Seminole Indians of Florida devised this form of patchwork in the late 1800s. It was a direct result of the invention of the sewing machine and hand-operated sewing machines were in Seminole camps in Southern Florida as early as 1880. This type of patchwork made economical use of cotton fabric scraps from the making of garments and served as a form of embellishment that replaced time-consuming hand appliqué. The Seminole patchwork appeared as horizontal strips in clothing that represented such concepts as a tree, fire, rain, or a man on a horse. Although this type of patchwork was traditionally done with solid colors, especially black and turquoise, the technique is well suited to borders, strip embellishments, and even a decorative trim on Christmas ornaments.

Supplies

Quilt borders, backing and binding

2½ yards batik or streaked fabric for border blocks

½ yard sashing fabric

2 yards inner and outer borders and binding fabric

4 yards backing fabric

69" x 71" piece of batting

Cut

▼ Border blocks: 4" strips cut into quarter-square triangles

▼ Sashing strips: 11 strips 1½" wide cut the length of the fabric. Cut 5 of these strips into 10" lengths.

▼ Inner border: 4 strips 2" wide cut the length of the fabric

▼ Outer border: 4 strips 3½" wide cut the length of the fabric

▼ Binding: 4 strips 2½" wide cut the length of the fabric

Supplies: Ornament blocks

1¼ yards white background fabric

16 assorted holiday fabrics (fat eighths, fat quarters, or scraps) for ornaments and patchwork

1 package medium-width metallic rickrack

1 package single-fold metallic bias tape

1 package or 1½ yards thin metallic braid or cording

Cut

▼ 16 background squares: 11" x 11"

▼ 16 sets of holiday ornament fabrics:
   2 strips of each fabric cut 3½" x 8"

Important note: The ornaments will be applied to these squares. Appliqué done by hand or machine tends to draw up the background fabric and change the dimensions. For this reason the background squares can be cut at least one inch larger (11" x 11") and trimmed to 10" x 10" after the ornaments have been stitched to the squares. When sewn to the sashing strips, the blocks will finish 9½" x 9½".

Seminole Patchwork Strips

For variety try both the three- and five-strip Seminole patchwork strips or experiment with different widths and placement of the strips.

All strips should be cut approximately 18" long.

Two-color or Three Strips:	Three-color or Five Strips:
1 center strip: 1" wide	1 center strip: ¾" wide
2 outer strips: 1½" wide	2 middle strips: 1" wide
	2 outer strips: 1½" wide

Directions

Sew the Seminole patchwork strips together using a ¼" seam allowance. Sew these strips with a shorter stitch length than normal because the resulting units will be cut into small segments (Fig. 1). Press the seams away from the center strip or to one side.

Fig. 1. Two narrow strips of fabric have been added to a strip of Seminole patchwork to create an interesting design for the center of this Christmas ornament.

Cut the sewn units into 1" segments (Fig. 2).

Sew the segments together aligning the lower seam of the center strip unit with the top seam of the center of the next segment (Fig. 3). Press the seams to one side or open if necessary to reduce bulk.

Trim the top and bottom of the Seminole patchwork strip leaving a ¼" seam allowance on both sides of the design. Place your ruler with the ¼" line along the top edge of the peaks or points of the outermost border fabric.

Sew the strip pairs of 3½" wide ornament fabric to the top and bottom of the Seminole patchwork strip. Press the seams away from the center.

Trace the pattern for the ornament on the dull side of a piece of freezer paper. Cut out the ornament on the traced line. Fold the ornament pattern in half vertically and horizontally as shown (Fig. 4). The one fold line should pass through the center of the ornament neck or cap. Mark these lines with a pencil. Iron the freezer paper onto the back of the ornament fabric, aligning the horizontal middle of the pattern with the middle of the Seminole strip.

Trim the fabrics leaving a ⅜" seam allowance beyond the paper pattern. Finger press the seam allowance to the back of the ornament. Clip the seam allowance in the neck area of the ornament. Baste the seam allowance to the back of the ornament and press.

Fold the background fabric in half both vertically and horizontally and finger press. Align the vertical

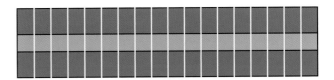

Fig. 2. Shown here is an example of a two-color or three-strip design to be cut into 1" segments.

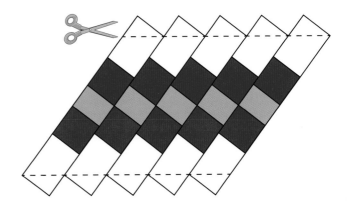

Fig. 3. The three-color or five-strip sample shows the pattern created when the cut segments are arranged by matching the center strip's lower seam with the top seam of the next center strip's seam.

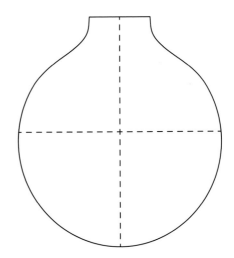

Fig. 4. Fold the ornament pattern in half both horizontally and vertically.

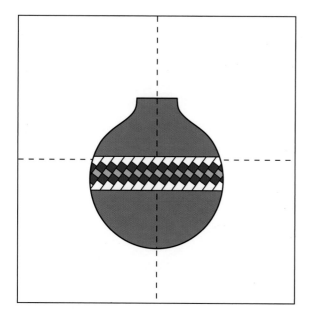

Fig. 5. Properly align each ornament on the background fabric.

Fig. 6. Form a graceful loop and pin the cording in place.

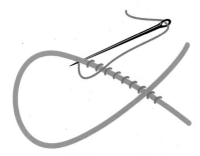

Fig. 7. Couching stitches should be approximately ⅛" apart.

center of the ornament with the center of the background fabric placing the ornament 2" above the bottom of the background fabric (Fig. 5).

Cut a 4" piece of narrow cording or braid. Cross the cut ends of the cord over themselves to form a loop and slip the ends under the neck of the ornament (Fig. 6). The location where the cord crosses itself should be positioned about ¼" under the top neck of the ornament.

Couch the cording in place (Fig. 7). Couching is a method used to secure or hold down cord, thick thread, or yarn with a thinner thread. The thread, cord, or yarn to be couched is laid along the design line or the desired location. Do not pin directly into the cording. Insert the pin ¼" before the cording and bring the point of the pin up again just in front of the edge of the cording. Insert the pin back into the background fabric on the other side of the cording. The center portion of the pin will cross over the top of the cording to hold it in place. Using a 50-weight matching thread, the needle is brought up on the design line or the base of the cord, thread, or yarn and inserted down into the background fabric just slightly above the previous entry point with the thread passing over the top of the couched thread, yarn, or cord. Repeat the stitches at ⅛" intervals.

Appliqué the ornament to the background fabric leaving a 2" opening at the bottom of the ornament. Remove the basting and pull the paper pattern out. Appliqué the opening closed.

To form the cap for the ornament, open the metallic bias tape and sew the rickrack centered along the bottom fold line of the bias tape with the right sides of both the rickrack and tape together. Fold along the stitching line with only the lower edge of the rickrack showing below the tape. Rather than trying to stitch short segments of rickrack and tape together, it is easier to stitch one yard pieces together before cutting the pieces for the caps of the ornaments. Cut a 1¾" segment of the tape and rickrack strip and fold under both ends. Pin the piece in place over the top neck of the ornament and appliqué on all sides using a matching thread.

Quilt Sashing and Borders

Following the quilt assembly as shown in Figure 8, arrange the 16 completed and trimmed 10" x 10" ornament blocks on a design wall in a pleasing arrangement with four blocks across and four blocks down. Stitch a sashing strip to the top and bottom of each of the four blocks in the top row. Stitch sashing strips to only the bottom of each block in the following three rows. Join the ornament blocks into four coulmns and press the seams toward the center of the sashing strips.

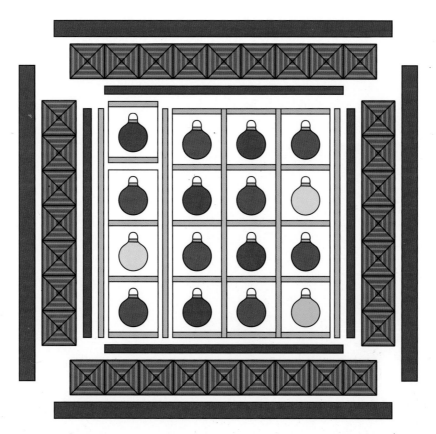

Fig. 8. Quarter-square triangles are used to form the blocks for the border of this holiday quilt.

Finished sizes:

Ornament block: 9½"

Streaked border block: 6½"

Sashing: 1"

Inner border: 1½"

Inner border: 3"

Sew a long sashing strip to both sides of the first and last columns. Sew another sashing strip to the right side of column two. Sew columns two and three together. Attach the first column to the unit that is made up of columns two and three. Stitch column four to the first three columns and press the seam allowances to the center of the sashing strips (Fig. 8, page 61).

Follow the Quilt Master Plan for constructing the batik or streaked border blocks. Trim these blocks to 7" to assure that they will fit the perimeter of the center of the quilt plus the inner border. Sew the inner borders to the top, bottom, and then to the sides of the quilt center. Join the batik blocks to form two units made of seven blocks and two units made of nine blocks. Stitch the seven-block units to the sides of the quilt center and stitch the nine-block units to the top and bottom. Press the seams away from the blocks. Stitch the 3½" outer border strips to the sides and then to the top and bottom of the quilt. Press the seams away from the batik or streaked blocks.

Construct the quilt backing incorporating any leftover ornament, sashing, and binding fabrics or two panels of two-yard backing fabric (Fig. 9). Select an appropriate quilting design for the borders and the area around the ornaments or echo quilt this area. Attach the binding and reserve this quilt for display during the holidays.

Fig. 9. ORNAMENTATION, back. The back of the quilt was made using fabric left over from constructing the quilt top. Note that the two extra blocks were incorporated into the quilt back.

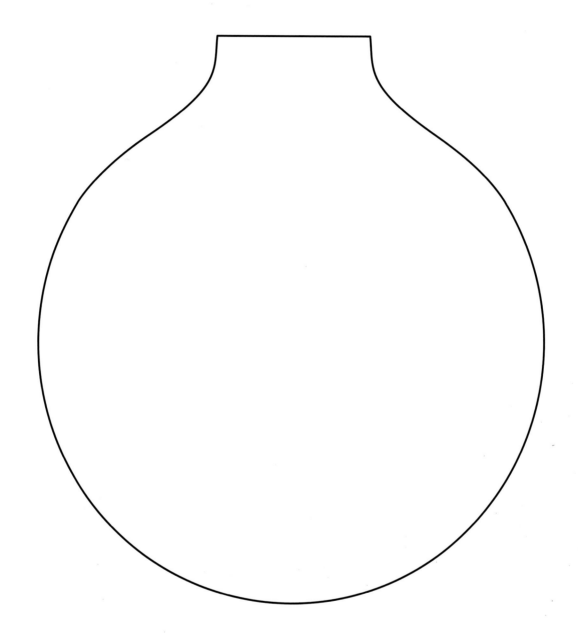

ORNAMENTATION, ornament
Shown at 100%

Piecing Border and Binding Strips

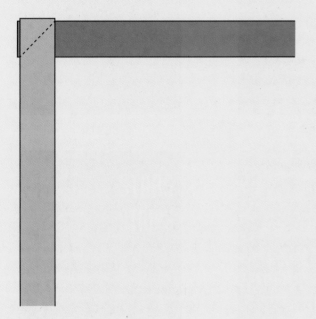

Use a diagonal seam to eliminate bulk when joining sashing, borders, and binding strips.

t is sometimes necessary to join strips of fabrics to form long borders and bindings. When fabric strips are joined using a diagonal seam, there is less bulk when the seam is pressed open and a smoother transition from piece to piece without an obvious horizontal ridge.

Place strips of fabric with the right sides together to form a 90-degree angle. Stitch diagonally from top to bottom intersecting edges to form a stitching line at a 45-degree angle as shown. Trim the fabric leaving a ¼" seam allowance. Press the seam open or to one side depending on the use of the strips and your preference. Experienced quilters believe that a seam pressed to one side is a stronger seam than one that has been pressed open. Open seams are flatter and create less bulk at the point at which they are joined. To ensure a strong seam when the seam is pressed open, use a shorter stitch length.

OPPOSITE: TWILIGHT, detail. Full quilt shown on page 77.

Sleeve for Hanging

The *Streaks of Batiks* technique is well suited to wall quilts and, if this is the intended end use of a quilt, a fabric sleeve should be attached to the top of the back of the quilt for hanging. The sleeve serves to protect the quilt's fabric from contact with a wood or metal rod and also evenly distributes the weight of the quilt along the full width of the quilt. Many how-to quilt books describe different techniques for creating a sleeve. If the quilt is to be entered in a quilt show or contest, the rules should be reviewed to determine the requirement for the sleeve width.

After a quilt has been quilted and before it is bound, a sleeve can easily be secured to the top by the machine stitching used to attach the binding and by hand stitching along the bottom fold of the sleeve. Cut a fabric strip 8½" wide and the width of the quilt from muslin or fabric leftover from constructing the quilt. Turn under the 8½" sides of the strip approximately ¼" twice so that there are no raw edges and the hem appears on the wrong side of the fabric.

With the wrong sides of the sleeve fabric together, fold the strip lengthwise with one cut edge ½" below the other edge. Press the bottom fold firmly to create a crease. Align the two cut edges of the strip with the wrong sides of the fabric together and stitch a scant ¼" seam. Place the sleeve's two raw edges along the top of the unbound quilt. The side of the sleeve with the shortest distance from the cut edge to the creased fold is to be placed facing the quilt and the longer edge with the extra fullness will face out. Note that the top section of the sleeve has extra fullness that will accommodate a round pole or rod. The sleeve should be approximately ½" from the side edges of the quilt. Baste the sleeve in place along the top edge. Bind the quilt as usual, catching the raw top edges of the sleeve and being careful not to bind the side edges of the sleeve.

Whipstitch the bottom folded edge of the binding to the back of the quilt being sure that your stitches do not show on the front of the quilt. Stitch the side edges of the sleeve to the quilt to prevent a rod from being inserted next to the actual quilt fabric.

There are other methods to create a sleeve for hanging quilts, but the author finds the method described to be the simplest. Another construction method will be necessary if the quilt is already bound or there is a possibility that the sleeve will need to be removed for some reason. It is important to remember that when applying a sleeve to a quilt that is already bound, the sleeve should be positioned ½" from the top bound edge and whipstitched in place. The bottom edge of the sleeve should be folded up ½" from the bottom fold and stitched to the back of the quilt. This will allow for fullness in the sleeve to accommodate a rod or pole for hanging.

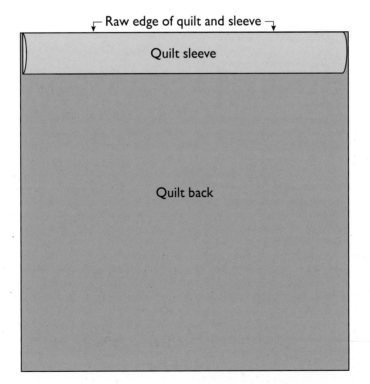

The raw edges of the sleeve are covered by the quilt's binding.

Binding the Quilt

Measure the top and one side of the quilt; double the combined measurements to take into account all four sides and add approximately 15" to the total. The additional 15" will allow extra binding for the corners and a diagonal seam to join the beginning and end of the binding. Cut enough 2½" lengthwise or crosswise grain strips to equal the desired length. Note that strips cut lengthwise will have less stretch than those that are cut horizontally or selvage-to-selvage. Join the strips with a diagonal seam as described in "Piecing Border and Binding Strips" on page 64. With the wrong sides of the fabric together, fold the strips in half along the full length of the strip and press.

After the quilt has been quilted, the excess backing fabric and batting must be trimmed even with the quilt top. With a rotary cutter and ruler, trim the batting and backing fabric, straighten the outer border fabrics to an even width, and square the corners of the quilt.

Determine the starting point for attaching the binding by loosely aligning the binding with the raw edges of the front of the quilt. The binding should be positioned so that the binding's diagonal seams avoid the corners of the quilt. The extra bulk of

LEFT: FUSION, detail. Full quilt shown on page 77.

Step A1

Step A2

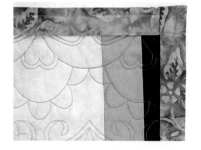

Step A3

Step A4. PHOTOS: CHARLES R. LYNCH

these seams will make it difficult to form flat mitered corners. Align the raw edges of the binding and the quilt, placing the binding strip on the right side of the quilt. Using a ¼" seam allowance, begin stitching approximately 10" from the beginning of the binding (Step A1).

It is possible to form neat mitered corners without cutting the binding strip. Stitch to within ¼" of the corner, stop, and backstitch about ⅜". Lift the needle and presser foot and rotate the quilt 90-degrees to align the quilt and attach the binding to the next side of the quilt. Position the binding above the previous line of stitching and parallel to the raw edges of the side of the quilt to be stitched (Step A2).

Fold the binding down on itself (Step A3) parallel and on top of the next side to be bound. This will form a fold that is positioned along the top edge of the previously stitched binding.

Backstitch and continue stitching a ¼" seam allowance to attach the binding to the quilt (Step A4).

Repeat steps A1 to A4 to form the miter at each of the next three corners.

Stop stitching approximately 10" from the binding's beginning stitches and remove the quilt from the sewing machine. Place the quilt right-side up on a flat surface and fold both binding ends back on themselves so the folds meet in the center of the unstitched area. Finger press these folds firmly to form a visible crease (Step B1).

Step B1

Open the loose ends of both pieces of the folded binding. On the wrong side of the fabric on each binding strip mark about 3" along the center fold and the vertical finger pressed line using a pencil, tailor's chalk, or other marker (Step B2).

Step B2

Place the ends of the binding strips perpendicular to each other with the right sides of the fabric together; insert a pin through the dissecting points of each binding piece forming right angles and matching the crease and center fold marked lines (Step B3).

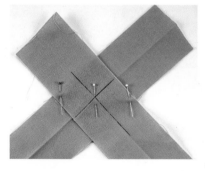

Step B3

Hint

Open the folded binding strips and pin along the proposed diagonal stitching line, matching the area of the center fold. Fold the binding in half and place it along the unstitched area of the quilt, checking to make sure that the proposed diagonal stitching line is at the proper angle and that the bottom edges of both binding strips align without twisting.

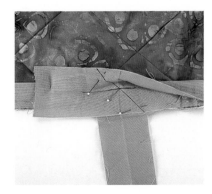

Step B4

Mark a 45-degree diagonal stitching line from binding edge to edge and dissecting the center point of the two marked lines (Step B4).

Once the alignment of the strips has been stitched, check again to be certain that the angle is correct and that there are no twists in the binding before trimming the seam allowance. Finger press the seam open and continue stitching the binding to the edge of the quilt (Step B5).

Step B5. PHOTOS: CHARLES R. LYNCH

Fold the binding to the back of the quilt using your machine stitching line as a guide and blindstitch the binding in place. The edges and the binding of a quilt are subjected to the most wear. The double layer of fabric in the binding and small hand stitches with good quality thread will extend the life of a quilt.

General Quilt Cleaning Directions

There are several university, quilt artist, and quilting organization websites that have a section devoted to the care and washing of antique and fine handmade quilts. One website sells labels that can be sewn to the back of the quilt that give instructions for cleaning a quilt. Advice is given on the type and brands of detergents to use and several offer suggestions on dealing with fabric dyes that are not colorfast and run. A full water level in the tub of the washer, color catcher sheets, or a piece of muslin can help disperse and absorb free dyes in the wash water.

Three things should always be emphasized when washing a quilt:

1. Wash quilts in cool or lukewarm water with a suitable detergent such as Orvus® or quilt soap.

2. Do not dry clean cotton quilts.

3. Never put a fine quilt in the clothes dryer.

The author uses a statement about the care of fine handmade quilts in a document that she includes with a quilt given as a gift. The document also gives information about the quiltmaker, the materials used in the quilt, the construction techniques, and the purpose for the gift.

Care Instructions:

The author always presents the person receiving the gift of a quilt with an information sheet. This document includes information about the maker of the quilt, materials used, construction techniques, the purpose for the gift, and care instructions. Note the care instructions at the end of the two sample documents, "Brynn Elizabeth Kleiner's Quilt," page 74 and "Jodhpur's Gift," page 75.

Duplicate the author's care instructions or create your own suggested washing and care instructions for the quilts that you give to others or donate. Include the following information in your instructions:

▼ Use cool or warm water and an appropriate detergent when washing the quilt.

▼ Never bleach or dry clean a fine cotton quilt.

▼ Avoid mechanical agitation of a quilt in a clothes washer or the dryer. Hand washing or soaking is a safer cleaning treatment. Always rinse quilts well to remove all traces of detergent.

▼ Keep fine quilts out of direct sunlight to prevent fading.

▼ Do not store quilts in plastic. Use a cotton pillowcase or old sheet to keep the quilt dust free and to prevent the quilt from coming into direct contact with wood, metal, or ordinary papers. A basement, damp, or hot area is not a suitable environment in which to store quilts.

Quilt Documentation

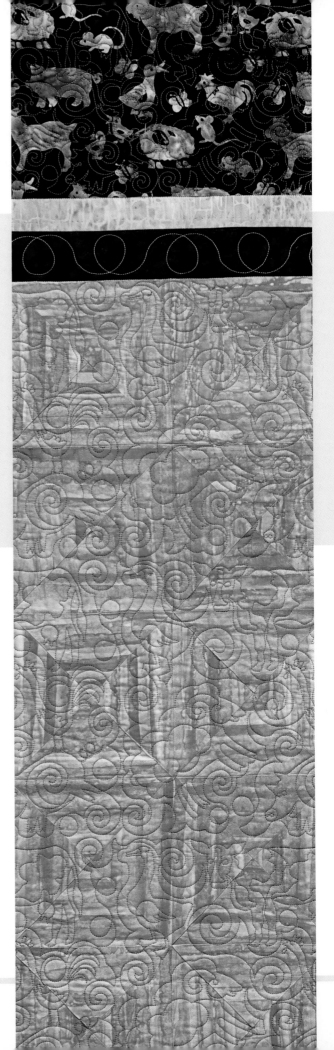

Often quilts are found in museums, books, and antique auctions in which the makers are described as anonymous or unknown. Experts can only estimate the age of the quilt by observing the fabrics, dyes, and prints as well as the style of the blocks or pattern design. Some patterns are associated with particular regions of the country and specific religious or ethnic groups, but because a quilt was found in one area of the country, it does not mean that it originated there. Without documentation, pertinent information such as the name of the quiltmaker, where it was made, date, and the purpose for which it was made can only be speculation.

Establishing provenance for a quilt is as simple as writing a one-page informational document. In addition to an embroidered, computer printed, or written label, further documentation can be appropriate. A computer-generated information sheet giving details about the purpose or occasion of the gift of a quilt, such as a wedding, birthday, graduation, birth of a baby, farewell, or token of appreciation, gives future generations the reason a quilt was made and by whom. A young couple to whom this quiltmaker gave a quilt for their new baby stated that they had placed the quilt's information sheet in their safety deposit box along with the deed to their house. It was important to them that this information be preserved.

Title the document using the quilt recipient's family name or the name of the organization to which the quilt is to be given, for example, "Kate Cutler Baby Quilt" or "Cummings School Quilt 2011." Create your own form and save the information in a computer folder to make other information sheets for future quilts. Include information about the quiltmaker and her or his relationship to the recipient. Mention any honors or awards the maker has received. The quilter's occupation and quilting experience add interest to the document. Simply change the first paragraph stating the purpose for the quilt and the other paragraph describing the fabric and construction techniques. The information regarding the quiltmaker and the care instructions will remain the same for each document. At the bottom of the sheet leave a space for the quilter's signature and include the maker's full name, place of residence, and date.

Do not miss the opportunity to educate the person receiving the quilt about the proper care of a handmade quilt. The information sheet given with each quilt should contain some guidelines for the correct cleaning methods for this textile product. Note the care instructions given in the two sample information documents that follow. Although it is impossible to govern the care, display, and cleaning of a quilt once it has been given, you can make suggestions regarding the storage and display of the quilt. I always inform the person receiving the quilt that if they would like to display the quilt as a wallhanging that I am willing to sew a sleeve or fabric tube to the back of the quilt for a rod. Advise the new quilt owner not to pin or tack the quilt to the wall because the weight of a quilt can cause tears or pins can rust. A cotton fabric sleeve hand sewn to the back of the quilt through which a dowel, curtain rod, or pole can be inserted is the proper way to hang a quilt.

Consider printing the information on a plain 8½" × 11" sheet of paper or enhance the presentation by printing the document on parchment or specialty paper available in single sheets at many craft and stationery stores. Fold the sheet as you would a business document or letter and insert it into a long envelope with the document's title printed on the envelope. Other options would be to print the information on paper to create a scroll or frame the information sheet to hang beside the quilt.

Of course, an informational sheet about a quilt is of little value if it is not kept with the quilt. It is possible to sew a fabric pocket on the back of the quilt to hold this document. Sometimes a pocket is made from scraps of fabric left over from constructing the quilt top and often contains other scraps of fabric with the intention that these fabrics be used for repairs to the quilt if this should become necessary.

BARNYARD, 54" × 54". The playful farm animals in the border fabric are duplicated in the pantograph chosen for quilting this child's quilt. Detail shown on opposite page. PHOTOS: CHARLES R. LYNCH

BRYNN ELIZABETH KLEINER'S QUILT

This crib quilt was made by Sandra Holzer of Adams, Massachusetts for the first child of Theresa and Bob Kleiner, Brynn Elizabeth Kleiner. Brynn was born on December 25, 2006 in Manchester, New Hampshire. Brynn's grandparents, Sandra and Richard Kleiner, are friends and neighbors of the quiltmaker.

The blue fabric with white rabbits called "Grounded in Love" printed by South Seas Imports is cotton and was selected because of Theresa's fondness for rabbits. The two-dimensional rabbits are constructed in segments and applied to or inserted into the pieced backing. All fabrics are 100 percent cotton and the batting is formed from bonded new polyester fibers. The machine quilting was done by Doryne Pederzani of Happy Valley Machine Quilting in Northampton, Massachusetts. Doryne stitched carrots in the green border and sunflowers in the outer borders to complement the print with clusters of rabbits performing varied tasks. She stitched a grass-like pattern in the border triangles, a series of circles in the sashing strips, and a linear design on the blocks of the quilt. Sandra and Doryne have a quilt featured in Karen McTavish's book *Mastering the Art of McTavishing*, published in 2005.

The quiltmaker is Sandra Brown Holzer of Adams, Massachusetts. Sandra has well over 200 quilts to her credit and is a former home economics teacher with a Master's degree in textiles and special education. Her teaching experience includes a six-year assignment for the Department of Defense in Bremerhaven, Germany. She is an avid quilter and longtime collector of textiles.

Care Instructions:

All quilts are best kept out of direct sunlight. Colors will fade and sunlight can weaken fibers. Quilts should be stored in a cool dry place without contact with wood, plastic, or regular papers. A bag or large pillowcase made from an old washed cotton sheet will protect the quilt from dust. If the quilt is folded, it should be refolded, varying the position of the folds, a couple of times each year. Handwash the quilt in Orvus®, quilt soap, or Woolite® in a tub of a top-loading washer in cool or warm water by soaking it for five minutes and using your hands to push the quilt up and down in the water. Do not let the machine agitate. Drain the washer with the quilt still in the tub and fill the tub again with clean water, push the quilt up and down with your hands, and let the quilt spin in the washer (no agitation) to remove excess water. Repeat the rinsing process and line dry the quilt by draping it over a series of ropes on a clothesline. Avoid direct sunlight when possible or place a clean lightweight sheet over the quilt. The quilt can also be placed on a clean sheet outside on the grass until it is dry. The use of a dryer and dry cleaning are not recommended for fine cotton quilts.

Sandra L. Holzer
Adams, Massachusetts
March 2007

JODHPUR'S GIFT

This quilt is given to the Cummings School of Veterinary Medicine at Tufts University by the Holzer family in appreciation for the care and treatment received by their Jack Russell Terrier, Jodhpurs (a.k.a. Jodie), by doctors and staff. It is through the efforts of these professionals that we came to realize that treatment does not necessarily require a cure, but a positive outcome can be quality of life and the animal owner's belief that decisions regarding the course of treatment were the right choices for their pet.

The theme fabric for the quilt is composed of a variety of animals. The fabric was designed by M. E. Hordyszynski for Michael Miller Fabrics, and all fabrics used in the quilt are 100 percent cotton. The quilt blocks were constructed by stacking four layers of identical fabric on top of each other and cutting strips. The strips were cut into squares and four identical squares were arranged and joined to form a block. The blocks were set on-point and bordered with a thin strip of Amish black fabric. The fabrics were washed before construction and the batting is 100 percent polyester. The back of the quilt is an abstract design created by using the remnants of fabrics used to construct the top of the quilt. The quiltmaker prefers the challenge of creating a pleasing design for the backs of her quilts rather than using a solid quilt-backing fabric or muslin. She intentionally underestimates the yardage necessary for the quilt backing when purchasing fabrics for her quilts.

The quiltmaker is Sandra Brown Holzer of Adams, Massachusetts. Sandra has well over 200 quilts to her credit and is a former home economics teacher with a Master's degree in textiles and special education. She is an avid quilter and longtime collector of textiles. Long arm quilter, Doryne Pederzani of Northampton, Massachusetts stitched a grass-like pattern in the border triangles, a series of circles in the sashing strips, and a linear design on the blocks of the quilt. Sandra and Doryne have a quilt featured in Karen McTavish's book, *Mastering the Art of McTavishing*, published in 2005.

Care Instructions:

All quilts are best kept out of direct sunlight. Colors will fade and sunlight can weaken fibers. Quilts should be stored in a cool dry place without contact with wood, plastic, or regular papers. A bag or large pillowcase made from an old washed cotton sheet will protect the quilt from dust. If the quilt is folded, it should be refolded, varying the position of the folds, a couple of times each year. Handwash the quilt in Orvus®, quilt soap, or Woolite® in a tub of a top-loading washer in cool or warm water by soaking it for five minutes and using your hands to push the quilt up and down in the water. Do not let the machine agitate. Drain the washer with the quilt still in the tub and fill the tub again with clean water, push the quilt up and down with your hands, and let the quilt spin in the washer (no agitation) to remove excess water. Repeat the rinsing process and line dry the quilt by draping it over a series of ropes on a clothesline. Avoid direct sunlight when possible or place a clean lightweight sheet over the quilt. The quilt can also be placed on a clean sheet outside on the grass until it is dry. The use of a dryer and dry cleaning are not recommended for fine cotton quilts.

Sandra L. Holzer, Adams, Massachusetts
February, 2009

Gallery

FIESTA, 52" x 52". A printed streaked fabric is used to create a dramatic wallhanging.

BEACH BALLS, 58" x 58". The circular-print border fabric gives a playful feel to this quilt with its monochromatic center color scheme.

UNDER THE MICROSCOPE, 58" x 58". The border fabric gives the illusion of the view of organisms when viewed under a microscope.

THE SHELL SEEKERS, 42" x 42". Made by Kathleen McGrath. She employed the quarter-square triangle technique to form the background for a silhouette of herself and her grandson on the beach. Enlarged from a photograph taken by her daughter.

FUSION, 80" x 102". Additional yardage can be used to create a queen- or king-size quilt.

TWILIGHT, 43" x 43". Made by by Betty King. A fabric printed with the images of tree trunks was used to make the blocks for this contemporary quilt.

CLUELESS, 35" x 35". Made by Kathleen McGrath. The *Streaks of Batiks* technique was used to create a background for this quilt with a holiday theme. Note the clever use of a partial frame around two sides of the quilt.

LEAVES AND VINES, 48" x 48". A pattern of leaves and vines created with wax when dying this batik fabric adds a linear flowing element to the fabric and detail for the blocks.

POPPIES, 49" x 43". The color-saturated batik formed a bold center for this quilt.

PHOTO: CHARLES R. LYNCH

SHERBET, 62" x 70". The colors in the center of the quilt are mimicked in the printed batik fabric used for the outer border. Detail is shown on opposite page.

SWIRLS, 54" x 54". This quilt is framed by two solid-color fabrics that were found in both the batik fabric center and border fabric.

BAMBOOZLED, 56" x 56". The linear print of bamboo shoots has been employed to present a sophisticated image using the *Streaks of Batiks* technique.

About the Author

The author, Sandra L. Holzer, has over thirty-five years of quilting experience as a quiltmaker, teacher, lecturer, and designer. She earned a Master's degree from Syracuse University in textiles and special education. Two years were spent teaching home economics in Stamford, Connecticut, followed by a six-year teaching assignment in Bremerhaven, Germany, for the United States Department of Defense. She is an avid collector of textiles and a former business owner of one of the largest uniform and linen rental companies in Western Massachusetts. With a quilting studio above a three-bay garage, her residence is a renovated 1778 New England farmhouse in Adams, Massachusetts that she shares with her husband, two dogs, and one old horse.

Although her career choices led her on two very different career paths, she always had an intense awareness of color and fascination with textiles. Wanting to reduce her ever-growing pile of fabric scraps and remnants and finding traditional quilt backings uninteresting, she experimented with test, orphan, and extra blocks and cut shapes from each quilt project to create fabric groupings to be included in the backs of her quilts. When arranging quarter-square triangles from a batik quilt, the author discovered that she could arrange four quarter-square triangles to create an interesting block. Friends and students soon suggested that she move those blocks and designs to the front of her quilts. The idea for the book *Streaks of Batiks* was born. The flexibility of the technique and the many design possibilities allowed the creation of a series of quilts using the technique for art quilts, background fabrics for appliqué, and quilt borders.

more AQS books

This is only a small selection of the books available from the American Quilter's Society. AQS books are known worldwide for timely topics, clear writing, beautiful color photos, and accurate illustrations and patterns. The following books are available from your local bookseller, quilt shop, or public library.

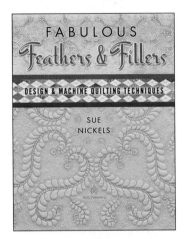

#1253

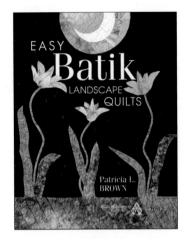

#8527

#8663

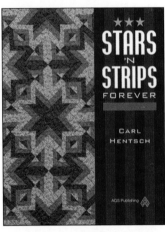

#1245

#1248

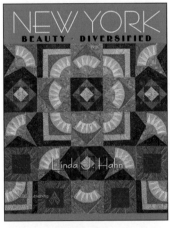

#1251

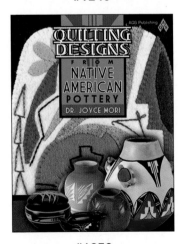

#1252

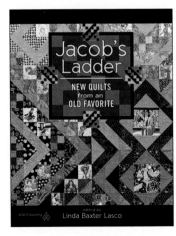

#1255

#1249

LOOK for these books nationally.
CALL or **VISIT** our website at

1-800-626-5420
www.AmericanQuilter.com